A RECORD OF
THE BUDDHIST COUNTRIES

by

Fa-hsien

(This English translation of Fa-hsien's *Record of Buddhist Countries* has been made by the San Shih Buddhist Institute, Peking, to commemorate the 2,500th anniversary of Buddha's Nirvana.)

THE CHINESE BUDDHIST ASSOCIATION
PEKING 1957

Translated from the Chinese

by

Li Yung-hsi

Printed in the People's Republic of China

Foreword
by Ho Chang-chun

Fa-hsien is one of China's great travellers, and the record of his journey to India in search of Buddhist canons is one of the earliest and most important travel accounts we possess. Now that Buddhists the world over are celebrating the two thousand five hundredth anniversary of the Nirvana of Sakyamuni Buddha, the founder of Buddhism, Fa-hsien's *Record of Buddhist Countries* which describes the early contacts between China and India deserves attention.

In the time of King Asoka (272-232 B.C.), Buddhism spread to Central Asia. By 128 B.C., when Emperor Wu of the Han dynasty sent Chang Chien* as his emissary to Central Asia, there was already a fair amount of trade between Bactria and India; and the fact that in Bactria Chang Chien saw bamboo sticks and cloth from western Szechuan, which had been brought from India to Central Asia, proves that there was traffic between southwest China and India either by sea or by the land route.

---

*In 138 B.C. Chang Chien was sent to Central Asia by Emperor Wu of the Han dynasty to persuade some of the rulers there to ally with China against the Huns. He visited Ferghana, Samarkand and Bactria.

As trade developed, the Buddhist religion spread. According to Chinese historical records, Buddhism was introduced into China proper during the reign of Emperor Ming (A.D. 58-75) of the Later Han dynasty. During the second century more Buddhist monks came to China from India and other Buddhist countries. In A.D. 147, for example, a monk named Lokaraksha or Lokaksin from Central Asia settled in Loyang, the capital of the Later Han dynasty; and other monks and devout laymen followed him from that region to propagate their religion. Quite probably their evangelizing zeal was the result of the promotion of Buddhism by the well-known monarch Kanishka.

During the second, third and fourth centuries, the foreign monks who came to China devoted most of their time to the translation of Buddhist canons. At least twenty-five Indian monks were engaged in this work before the time of Fa-hsien, and such men made an important contribution to the cultural exchange between India and China. From the beginning of the second to the end of the fourteenth century, according to existing records, more than two hundred monks came to China from Buddhist countries to translate Buddhist sutras.

The flourishing caravan trade of that time greatly helped the spread of Buddhism. For instance, Buddhayasa, a native of Kashmir who returned to his own country after translating Buddhist canons with Kumarajiva in Changan, sent a copy of a certain sutra with a caravan to Liangchow for translation into Chinese. Fa-tu, the famous fifth century monk, was the son of an Indian merchant who travelled for many years between India and Canton. Fa-tu himself was born in the province of Kiangsi. And Fa-hsien, when in Ceylon, saw a white silk Chinese fan which had got there through some merchant. Many other facts could be cited to show that there was considerable trading by land and sea between China and her western neighbours, and this facilitated the spread of Buddhism eastwards.

Most of the earliest Buddhist canons which reached China came from Central Asian kingdoms and not directly from India, many through Chinese Turkestan by way of Khotan on the south route, or Kucha on the north route. At the time these were important centres of Buddhism. However, the Buddhist canons brought to China during this period could not satisfy the needs of the Chinese monks, who wanted to make a thorough study of Buddhism. This is one reason why Chinese Buddhists risked their lives and endured great hardships to make the journey to India in search of additional sutras. Another reason was the rapid growth of Buddhism in China at this time. The number of monks had increased and the monasteries were growing, therefore Buddhists all over China felt an urgent need for additional Monastic Rules.

Fa-hsien's main purpose in travelling westwards was to seek for Monastic Rules in India. Chinese monks before him who journeyed in search of Buddhist sutras had gone no further than North India; but when Fa-hsien went there, he found that the monks there handed down their precepts orally and had no written records, so he pressed on to Central India. For the aim of his journey was not simply to make a pilgrimage to the land of Buddha nor to seek Buddhist teachers, but to obtain the Monastic Rules and sutras so urgently needed by his fellow monks. On his return to China, he was so eager to translate these documents as quickly as possible that instead of going to Changan to rejoin his former teachers and companions, as he had first intended, he went to Chienkang (Nanking) where he translated the sutras with the help of the Indian monk Buddhabhadra.

Fa-hsien's original name was Kung. He was admitted to the Buddhist order at the age of three and was given the religious name Fa-hsien (Law Manifest). He was already sixty-five when he set out from Changan in A.D. 399, accompanied by nine or ten other monks. He crossed deserts and the Pamir Plateau, travelled through North, Central and East India, down to South India, Ceylon and Sumatra, then sailed across the Indian Ocean and the China Sea, landed at Laoshan in the Shantung Peninsula, and reached Chienkang in A.D. 413. Of his companions, some had turned back, some had died, and some had remained in India Fa-hsien alone was single-minded enough to press on and overcome all difficulties. He was seventy-nine by the time he finally made his way back to China.

In A.D. 414, the year after his return to Chienkang, he wrote the record of his travels; and later, by request, added certain material to make the version which we have today. His *Record of Buddhist Countries,* also known as the *Travels of Fa-hsien,* gives a complete description of his journey and is the earliest comprehensive account we possess of the customs, geography and history of Central Asia, India and the Indian Ocean. This is a great travel book comparable to the later *Record of the Western Regions* by the monk Hsuan-chuang (Tripitaka) of the Tang dynasty.

Fa-hsien went to India during the reign of King Chandragupta II, also known as Vikramaditya. This was the most prosperous period of the Gupta dynasty; but apart from a few works of sculpture and some coins, the *Record of Buddhist Countries* is probably the only historical account left of that age. Fa-hsien's descriptions of the stone pillars inscribed with Asoka's decrees, and the other sculpture of that time, provide extremely useful material for research into King Asoka's reign. Similarly, he described many of the Buddhist monuments left by King Kanishka in northern India, which were still in good condition when he saw them. Again, we know that Fa-hsien strictly observed the Buddhist practice of remaining in retirement during the summer or rainy season, and from this and certain statements made by Hsuan-chuang, we can deduce a number of differences between the Chinese and Indian calendars. Fa-hsien's attitude towards Mahayana and Hinayana Buddhism also deserves attention; while the places he names in Central Asia, India and the Indian Ocean are of great interest to all who study the trade routes between China and the west and the geography of that region. Above all, his account helps us to understand conditions in many countries in Central Asia and India during the fourth and fifth centuries. Thus Fa-hsien's *Record of Buddhist Countries* is not simply one of the chief travel accounts in Chinese literature, but is of great interest also to historians and the general reader.

This well-known Chinese classic has been published in over twenty official and private editions since the Sung dynasty. Of the editions extant today the most important are: the Northern Sung edition from Tung Chan Monastery, Foochow, A.D. 1104; the Northern Sung edition from Kai Yuan Monastery, Foochow, A.D. 1148; the Southern Sung edition from Ssuhsi, Huchow, Chekiang, A.D. 1239; the Korean edition of 1246; and the various Ming editions dating from the seventeenth century; another Northern Sung edition was discovered in recent years in Kuang Sheng Monastery, Chaocheng, in Shansi.

Translations of this book include the French translation made by Abel-Rémusat in 1836, the English versions translated by S. Beal in 1869, by H. A. Giles in 1877, by James Legge in 1886, and a further rendering by Giles in 1923. The Japanese scholar Kiroku Adachi published an annotated text with the results of his researches in 1936, and a revised edition in 1940. We are indebted to the labours of all these sinologues.

CONTENTS*

*There is no division into sections in the original. These section titles have been provided by the translator for the convenience of readers.

Postscript by Another Monk

1. The Cause of the Journey

When living in Changan, Fa-hsien was distressed to observe that not all the canon of the Monastic Rules* was obtainable in China. For this reason, in the first year of Hung Shih (A.D. 399), the cyclic year of Chi Hai, he set out for India with his friends Hui-ching, Tao-chen, Hui-ying and Hui-wei, to seek for the Monastic Rules and regulations.

2. The Country of King Ju Tan and the Town of Changyeh

Setting out from Changan, they crossed the Lung Mountains and reached the country of King Chien Kuei, where they stayed for the summer retirement.** When the summer retirement was over, they proceeded to the country of King Ju Tan and, after crossing the Yang Lou Mountain, reached the garrison town of

---

*The *Vinaya-pitaka*. The Buddhist canons are divided into three main parts: the *Sutra-pitaka* (*Basket of Discourse*), containing the sayings of Buddha and his chief disciples, the *Vinaya-pitaka* (*Basket of Monastic Rules*); and the *Abhidharma-pitaka* (*Basket of Commentaries*).

**It was the Buddhist custom for monks to remain in retirement during the summer or rainy season.

Changyeh. Since there was great unrest there at the time and the roads were impassable, Tuan Yeh, the king of Changyeh, kept them there and acted as their patron. Thus they met Chih-yen, Hui-chien, Seng-shao, Pao-yun and Seng-ching; and, pleased to find that they shared one common purpose, they spent the summer retirement together.

3. Tunhuang

When the summer retirement was over they proceeded to Tunhuang, where there are fortifications about eighty *li* from east to west and forty *li* from south to north. After staying there for little more than a month, Fa-hsien and four others, five monks in all, set out in advance with a guide, leaving Pao-yun and the rest. Li Hao, the prefect of Tunhuang, provided them with the means to cross the desert. In this desert there are evil spirits and hot winds that kill every man who encounters them. No birds fly there and no beasts roam. As far as the eye can see, no road is visible across the desert, and only the skeletons of those who have perished there serve to mark the way.

4. The Country of Shenshen

After travelling for seventeen days and covering about 1,500 *li*, they reached the country of Shenshen. This land is rugged and barren, and its inhabitants dress much the same as in China, except that their clothes are made of felt. The king has embraced the Buddhist faith and this country has some 4,000 monks of the Hinayana School. The laity and monks here all practise the religion of India, but some observe it more strictly and some less so. This is the case in all the lands that they passed through on their way to the west, only the languages differ in each country; however, all the monks study Indian books and the Indian language.

5. The Country of Agni

Having stayed in Shenshen for more than one month, they travelled on northwest for fifteen days till they came to the country of Agni. Here there are also about 4,000 monks of the Hinayana School, who live strictly according to the Monastic Rules. Monks coming here from China are not permitted to take part in their rites. Fa-hsien was entertained here for more than two months by Fu Kung-sun, a Chinese monk, till he was rejoined by Pao-yun and the others.

As the people of Agni were lacking in courtesy and treated their guests rather coolly, Chih-yen, Hui-chien and Hui-wei returned to Karashar to procure necessities for the journey, while Fa-hsien and the others, with supplies provided by Fu Kung-sun, proceeded directly southwest. Because there are no inhabitants along the way, travelling in the desert is extremely difficult. Nothing in the world can compare with the hardships which they endured. But after a journey of one month and five days they reached Khotan.

6. The Country of Khotan and the Image Procession

This country is rich and happy, with a prosperous people. All its inhabitants are Buddhists, who delight in their religion. The number of monks amounts to several tens of thousands, most of whom study Mahayana Buddhism, and all of whom have food provided for them. The houses here are scattered, and a small stupa is built in front of each, from twenty feet upwards in height. There are dwelling places for monks, and provision is made to entertain monks from elsewhere. The king of this country lodged Fa-hsien and his party in a monastery called Gomati, of the Mahayana School. Here 3,000 monks live together, and assemble for meals at the sound of a bell. When they enter the refectory, they behave with sober propriety and take their seats in due order. All is quiet and there is no rattle of bowls. Instead of calling out when they want their bowls refilled, they simply sign with their fingers to the attendants.

Hui-ching, Tao-chen and Hui-ta went on ahead to Khalcha, while Fa-hsien and the others remained behind for another three months to see the image procession. Khotan has fourteen large monasteries, to say nothing of smaller ones. Beginning from the first day of the fourth month, the streets and lanes of the city are swept clean and decorated, while a great canopy, lavishly adorned, is erected above the city gate. Here the king and queen stay with their maids of honour. The monks of Gomati Monastery, being Mahayana monks whom the king respects, are the first to bear images in this procession. Three or four *li* from the city they make a four-wheeled image car in the shape of a movable palace, more than thirty feet high, which is adorned with the seven precious substances* and hung with silk pennants and canopies. Buddha's image stands in the centre of the car attended by two Bodhisattvas, while devas** of gold and silver or carved jade are suspended in the air. When the image has approached to within about a hundred paces of the gate, the king takes off his crown and changes into new clothes. Carrying flowers and incense, and followed by his attendants, he goes out of the city barefoot to receive the images, then pays homage at their feet, scattering the flowers and burning the incense before them. As the images enter the city, the queen and her maids on the gate-tower cast down all kinds of blossoms. There are different kinds of car for each ceremonial; and each monastery has one day to parade its images, the procession beginning on the first of the fourth month and ending on the fourteenth. After the

---

*Gold, silver, lapis-lazuli, crystal, beryl, emerald, and agate.
**Divinities of Indian mythology.

procession is completed, the king and queen return to their palace.

Seven or eight *li* to the west of this city is a monastery by the name of New Royal Monastery. Its construction took eighty years and three reigns to complete. Some two hundred feet high, it is ornamented with carvings and inlaid work, and studded with gold, silver and all kinds of jewels. Behind the stupa stands a magnificent and beautiful shrine-hall to Buddha, the beams, pillars, doors and windows of which are plated with gold. There are also monks' dwellings which are so splendid and richly adorned that no words can describe them. The kings of the six countries east of the Pamirs have presented many of their most costly jewels, seldom used by the common people, as offerings to this monastery.

7.   The Countries of Chakuka and Agzi

After the image procession in the fourth month, Seng-shao set out with a foreign monk for Kashmira, while Fa-hsien and the others proceeded towards Chakuka, which they reached after a journey of twenty-five days. The king of Chakuka is a devout Buddhist, and there are 1,000 monks or more, most of whom study Mahayana Buddhism. Having stayed here for fifteen days, they travelled southward for four days into the Pamirs, till they came to the country of Agzi, where they spent their summer retirement.

8. Khalcha and the Great Five Year Assembly

After the summer retirement they travelled north for twenty-five days to Khalcha, where they met Hui-ching and others.

At this time, the King of Khalcha was holding the *Panchavarsha,* or Great Five Year Assembly, and monks from the four quarters were invited here to take part. When the monks have assembled, their seats are adorned with silk streamers and canopies, as well as golden and silver lotus flowers, and clean cushions are provided. The king and his ministers make offerings to the monks according to the Buddhist custom for one, two or three months, generally in spring. After making his offerings, the king advises his ministers to present offerings for one, two, three or five days. When all the offerings have been made, the king bids one of his nobles ride a horse from his own stable, saddled with his own saddle, bearing white cloth, all kinds of jewels, and such things as are needed by monks, which he vows with his ministers to offer as alms. These offerings to the monks are later redeemed from them.

Khalcha is hilly and cold, and no grain but wheat will ripen there. The weather often turns frosty as soon as the monks have received their yearly offerings: so the king usually requests them not to receive these till after the wheat has ripened. In this country there is a stone spittoon once used by Buddha, of the same colour as the Blessed One's alms-bowl. Another relic is one of Buddha's teeth, for which the people here have built a stupa. There are more than a thousand monks, all of whom belong to the Hinayana School. To the east of these hills the people dress like the Chinese, except that they wear felt or serge. The various rules and ceremonies of the monks are too numerous to describe. This country is in the middle of the Pamirs and from this point onwards all the plants, trees and fruit are different from those of China, excepting only the bamboo, pomegranate and sugar-cane.

9. The Pamirs and the Country of Darada

From here they journeyed westward to North India, taking one month to cross the Pamirs, where there is snow in summer as well as winter. There are also venomous dragons which, when incensed, will breathe out pestilential wind, rain and snow, or cause most fearful sand-storms. Not one man in ten thousand can escape from these with his life. The local people are known as the Men of the Snow Mountains.

After crossing the Pamirs, they reached North India, and arrived at a small country on its borders called Darada. Here are also many monks, all of whom study Hinayana Buddhism.

In this country there was once an Arhat who, by the use of supernatural powers, sent a skilful sculptor up to the Tusita Heaven* to observe the proportions

---

*One of the thirty-three heavens in Indian mythology. Tusita means "Satisfied."

22

and features of Maitreya Bodhisattva, so that on descending to earth he could carve an image of Maitreya in wood. The sculptor completed the image after three ascents to heaven to make observations. Eighty feet high and eight feet broad at the base, the statue often radiates light on fast days. The kings of many countries vie with each other in making offerings to it, and it has remained in Darada to this day.

10. The Dangerous Crossing

They travelled southwest through the Pamirs for fifteen days, meeting many obstacles on the road, which is very hard to travel, and many dangerous precipices. The crags rise sheer to a formidable height. If a man looks down he becomes dizzy, and if he wishes to go forward he can find no foothold. Below flows a river by the name of Indus. The ancients hewed a path here out of the rocks like a stairway with seven hundred steps. After passing this stairway, they crossed the river by a rope suspension bridge. The banks of the Indus are nearly eighty paces apart. This place is so far from China that they had encountered nine different languages on the way. Even Chang Chien and Kan Ying* of the Han dynasty never went as far as this.

---

*Sent as an imperial envoy to Central Asia in A.D. 97, Kan Ying visited Parthia and other kingdoms.

The monks of this country asked Fa-hsien, "Do you know when Buddhism was first introduced to the East?"

"I have asked people there," replied Fa-hsien, "and they all agree that it was introduced long ago. Since Maitreya's image was set up, Indian monks have continuously crossed this river with Buddhist scriptures and books of monastic discipline. The image was set up about three hundred years after Buddha's Nirvana, which corresponds roughly to the time of King Ping* of the Chou dynasty. So we may say that the spread of the Great Religion dates from the time of that statue. If Maitreya Bodhisattva had not succeeded Sakyamuni Buddha, who else would have caused the Three Precious Gems** to spread and enabled the frontier peoples to understand the Law? We may be sure that the beginning of this mystery was not the work of men, and there must be a reason for the dream of Emperor Ming of the Han dynasty."***

After crossing the Indus River they arrived at the country of Udyana.

---

*770-720 B.C.

**Buddha, Dharma (the Law), and Sangha (the Buddhist order).

***A.D. 58-75. The emperor dreamed that he saw a divine figure radiating light. When he awoke and questioned his ministers, one of them told him that this was Buddha. Then the emperor sent envoys to the western regions to seek for Buddhism, and in A.D. 67 they brought back two monks who introduced Buddhism to China.

11. The Country of Udyana

The country of Udyana is the northernmost part of India, but all its inhabitants speak the language of Central India, which is known as the Middle Kingdom. The laymen's clothes and food are also the same as in the Middle Kingdom, and Buddhism flourishes here. They call the places where monks stay *sangharamas,* or monasteries, and here are five hundred *sangharamas,* all of the Hinayana School. If a monk from elsewhere arrives, he is entertained for three days, after which he is asked to find lodgings for himself.

Tradition has it that Buddha came to this country when he visited North India. He left a footprint here, which is long or short according to the understanding of whoever looks at it — this is still so today. The rock on which Buddha sunned his robe and converted an evil dragon is also there to this day. This rock is fourteen feet high and about twenty feet wide. One side of it is smooth.

Hui-ching, Tao-chen and Hui-ta, these three, went on ahead to the country of Nagarahara, where there is a shadow of Buddha, while Fa-hsien and the others remained in Udyana for the summer retirement.

12. The Country of Suvastu

After the summer retirement, they went south to the country of Suvastu, where Buddhism also flourishes. This is where Lord Sakra in former days tested Buddha by transforming himself into a hawk and a dove, and to ransom the dove Buddha cut off a piece of his own flesh for the hawk. After Buddha attained to Buddha-hood, he came here with his disciples and told them: "During a former life, I cut off my flesh here to ransom a dove." So the people of Suvastu learnt of this, and built a stupa here, adorned with ornaments of gold and silver.

13. The Country of Gandhara

Proceeding east for five days from here, they arrived at the country of Gandhara, which was formerly the kingdom of King Asoka's son Dharmavardhana. When Buddha was a Bodhisattva, he plucked out his eyes here and gave them as alms. A large stupa was built at this spot, adorned with gold and silver. Most of the people of this country study Hinayana Buddhism.

14. The Country of Takshasila

Travelling eastward from here for seven days, they reached the country called Takshasila, which means "decapitation." When Buddha was a Bodhisattva, he gave his head as alms here, and hence this name arose.

Going eastward again for two days, they came to the place where Buddha gave his body to feed a starving tiger. At both these places large stupas have also been built and embellished with many precious things. The kings, ministers and people of many countries vie with one another in making offerings, scattering flowers and lighting lamps at these stupas without intermission. These two stupas and the two mentioned before are called The Four Great Stupas by the people of Takshasila.

15. The Country of Purushapura and Buddha's Alms-bowl

Travelling south from Gandhara for four days, they reached the country of Purushapura. When Buddha was wandering here with his disciples, he said to Ananda, "After my Nirvana, a king by the name of Kanishka will build a stupa here."

When King Kanishka was later born into the world, he went on a pleasure trip; and Sakra, wishing to enlighten him, changed himself into a young cowherd who was building a stupa by the roadside.

"What are you doing?" asked the king.

"I am building a stupa for Buddha," replied the boy.

"Excellent!" said the king.

Then the king built a stupa more than four hundred feet high directly above the one the boy had built, and adorned it with all manner of precious things. None of the stupas and temples that they had seen on their way could compare with this in magnificence and stateliness, and it was generally said that this was the finest stupa in the whole of Jambudvipa.* When Kanishka had completed the construction of this stupa, the smaller one, which was roughly three feet high, emerged from the larger one on the south side.

Buddha's alms-bowl is in Purushapura. Formerly a king of the Sakas raised a great force to attack this country in order to carry off the bowl. Having conquered Purushapura, the Saka king, himself an ardent Buddhist, prepared great offerings and made ready to take the alms-bowl away. After presenting offerings to the Three Precious Gems, he caparisoned a great elephant and placed the bowl upon it; but the elephant crouched on the ground and could not move. He then made a four-wheeled cart to carry the bowl, with eight elephants to draw it, but again they could not move. Then the king understood that the time had not yet come for him to own the bowl. Filled with shame and regret, he built a stupa and monastery at the spot, posted a satrap there and made all manner of offerings.

There are about seven hundred monks here. When it is nearly noon, before their mid-day meal, the monks bring out the bowl so that laymen may make every kind of offering. In the evening they bring it out again when they burn incense. This bowl can hold about two pecks and is of various colours, but

---

*The ancient Indians believed that the world consisted of four continents, the continent in the south being Jambudvipa, or India.

black predominates. Its four layers are clearly apparent,* it is roughly a fifth of an inch thick, and it has a brilliant lustre. When a poor man puts a few flowers into it, the flowers fill the bowl; but a rich man who wishes to offer more cannot fill it even with a hundred, a thousand or ten thousand bushels of flowers.

After presenting offerings to Buddha's alms-bowl, Pao-yun and Seng-ching started home. Hui-ching, Hui-ta and Tao-chen had set out ahead of the others to the country of Nagarahara to make offerings to Buddha's shadow, tooth and skull; but Hui-ching fell ill there and Tao-chen remained to nurse him. Hui-ta returned alone to Purushapura to rejoin the others, and returned with Pao-yun and Seng-ching to China. Then Hui-ching died in Buddha's Bowl Monastery, and Fa-hsien proceeded alone to the temple of Buddha's skull.

16. The City of Hilo and Buddha's Skull

Travelling west for sixteen *yojanas*,** he reached the city of Hilo on the border of Nagarahara. In this city there is a temple for Buddha's skull, the whole of it plated with gold and adorned with the seven precious substances. The king of this country, out of respect for the skull and fear lest it be stolen, has appointed

---

*This bowl was made out of four alms-bowls given to Buddha.

**A *yojana* was regarded as a day's march for the army, but in Buddhist canons it is sometimes as little as five miles.

eight men of noble families, each with a seal, to seal up the temple in order to safeguard the relic. Early each morning, before the door is opened, these eight men go to make sure that their seals have not been tampered with. After the door has been opened, they wash their hands with scented water, bring Buddha's skull out of the temple and place it on a high throne. It is set on a circular stand made of the seven precious substances and covered with a glass bowl, all these objects being adorned with pearls and gems. The skull is a pale yellow, about four inches across and with a lofty cranium. Every day when it is taken out, the people in that temple ascend a high tower to beat a great drum, blow the conch and strike cymbals. When the king hears this, he goes to the temple to offer flowers and incense. After making his offerings, he worships the skull and goes away. He enters by the east gate and leaves by the west, making the same offering and worshipping every morning before attending to affairs of state. The laymen and elders also make their offerings before attending to their household affairs. This is the case every morning, nor is there any negligence. After all the offerings have been made, the skull is returned to the temple. It is kept in the Stupa of Emancipation, which is about five feet high, is made of the seven precious substances, and can be opened and closed. Before the gate of the temple every morning there are vendors of flowers and incense, and those who wish to make offerings can buy from them. The kings of many countries often send deputies to make offerings too. The site of this temple is about forty paces square, and it never stirs even during thunderstorms and earthquakes.

17. The Country of Nagarahara and Buddha's Shadow

Proceeding northward for one *yojana*, Fa-hsien reached the capital of Nagarahara. This is where the Bodhisattva once bought five flowers with silver coins to offer to Dipankara Buddha.* Here is also a stupa for Buddha's tooth, which is worshipped in the same way as the skull.

One *yojana* northeast of this city, he came to a valley where a temple has been built for the worship of Buddha's staff. The staff is of *gosirsha* sandalwood,** and sixteen or seventeen feet long. It is kept in a long wooden case, and not even a hundred or a thousand men can move it.

After entering the valley, he walked for four days towards the west till he came to the temple where offerings are made to Buddha's robe. If there is a drought in this land, the people bring out the robe to worship and present offerings to it; and then a heavy rain falls.

---

*The "illuminating Buddha," the twenty-fourth predecessor of Sakyamuni.

**The finest variety of sandalwood.

Half a *yojana* south of the city of Nagarahara, on the southwest side of a high mountain, is a cave where Buddha left his shadow. At a distance of ten paces or so, this shadow looks exactly like the true Buddha, with golden features which radiate brilliant light. When you go nearer, however, it becomes less distinct and seems only a blurred likeness. The kings of many countries have sent skilful artists to copy it, but none has succeeded in doing so. It is said that all the thousand Buddhas will leave their shadows in this cave.

About a hundred paces to the west of the shadow is a place where Buddha, while on earth, shaved his head and pared his nails. There Buddha and his disciples built a stupa from seventy to eighty feet high, which is standing to this day, as a model for future stupas. Beside it there is a monastery in which live some seven hundred monks. As many as a thousand stupas have been built here in honour of the various Arhats and Pratyeka Buddhas.*

18. The Lesser Snow Mountains and the Countries of Lakki, Harana and Uchcha

After staying in Nagarahara for three months during the winter, Fa-hsien and his two companions struck south across the Lesser Snow Mountains which are covered with snow in summer as well as winter. As

---

*Saints who attain to Buddha-hood individually, that is, without a teacher, and without being able to save others.

they were climbing the northern side of the mountains, which has no sun, sudden icy blasts swept down and made them shiver. White foam began to issue from Hui-ching's mouth, and he could go no further.

"It is all up with me," he said to Fa-hsien. "But you go on. Don't stay here to perish with me!"

And thereupon he died. Fa-hsien caressed him, lamenting bitterly.

"You have failed in your purpose!" he cried. "Yet such is fate!"

They gathered their remaining strength to push forward again and, proceeding to the south side of the mountains, reached the country of Lakki. Here they found about 3,000 monks of both the Mahayana and Hinayana Schools. And here they stayed for the summer retirement. The summer over, they descended into the valley to the south, and walked for ten days till they came to the country of Harana. Here there are also about 3,000 monks, all of whom study Hinayana Buddhism.

Journeying eastward for three days, they re-crossed the Indus River where the ground is smooth and level on both sides. Beyond the river lies the country called Uchcha. Buddhism flourishes here and both the Mahayana and Hinayana Schools are studied. On seeing two monks from China, the people of that country were greatly moved.

"How is it that men from across the border will leave their homes for the sake of the Law and come so far to seek Buddhism?" they demanded.

They therefore provided them with all that they needed, and entertained them according to Buddhist customs.

19. The Country of Mathura

Travelling southeast for nearly eighty *yojanas,* they passed a great number of monasteries with some ten thousand monks altogether. Having passed all these, they reached a country called Mathura where, once again, they crossed the Yamuna River. On the right and left sides of the river are twenty monasteries with some 3,000 monks. Buddhism flourishes there. All the kings of the Indian countries west of the Desert of Lop are devout believers in Buddha's Law. When making offerings to monks they take off their crowns and, with the members of the royal house and their ministers, serve food to the monks with their own hands. This done, they spread a carpet on the ground and sit down on it in front of the principal monk. They dare not sit on couches in the presence of monks. The rules for this making of offerings by kings have been handed down from the time of Buddha till now.

20. The Climate and Customs of the Middle Kingdom

The region to the south is known as the Middle Kingdom. The climate is temperate without frost or snow. The people are rich and contented, unencumbered by any poll-tax or official restrictions. Only those who till the king's land pay a land tax, and they are free to go or stay as they please. The kings govern without recourse to capital punishment, but offenders are fined lightly or heavily according to the nature of their crime. Even those who plot high treason only have their right hands cut off. The king's attendants, guards and retainers all receive emoluments and pensions. The people of this country kill no living creatures, drink no wine, and eat no onion or garlic. The single exception to this is the Chandalas, who are known as "evil men" and are segregated from the others. When they enter towns or markets they strike a piece of wood to announce their presence, so that others may know they are coming and avoid them. Neither pigs nor fowl are kept in this country and no living creatures are sold. There are no butchers or wine-sellers in the markets. Shells are used as currency in trading. Only the Chandala fishermen and hunters sell flesh.

After Buddha's Nirvana, the kings, elders and lay Buddhists built monasteries for the monks and provided them with houses, gardens, and fields, as well as with husbandmen and cattle to cultivate their land. Title-deeds inscribed on iron were handed down from king to king, and since none dared to annul them they are still in force. The monasteries are supplied with beds and bedding, food, drink and clothes, so that the monks want for nothing. This is the case everywhere. The monks devote themselves to practising virtue, reciting the scriptures or sitting in meditation. When a monk from elsewhere arrives, the resident monks welcome him and carry his robes and alms-bowl for him. They also bring water to wash his feet and oil to anoint them, and offer him a collation.* After he has rested, they ask him how long he has been ordained and provide him with a room, bedding and other things according to Buddhist Law.

Wherever monks live they build stupas in honour of the saints Sariputra, Maudgalaputra and Ananda,** also in honour of the Abbidharma or Buddhist Commentaries, the Monastic Rules and the Sutras. A month after the summer retirement, all devout families collect offerings for the monks and supply them with collations, while the monks hold a great assembly to expound the Law. The assembly at an end, they offer all manner of incense and flowers at the stupa of Sariputra, and keep the lamps there burning throughout the night. Actors are hired to perform a play in which Sariputra, who was originally a Brahman, goes to Buddha to ask for ordination. The lives of Maudgalaputra and Kasyapa are also performed in this way.

Most nuns present offerings at the Stupa of Ananda, for it was he who entreated Buddha to allow women to take orders. The novices for the most part present offerings to Rahula, the teachers of the Buddhist

---

*According to Buddhist rule, one should take no meal after noon. One could, however, partake of light refreshments such as honey or fruit juice.

**Three disciples of Buddha.

Commentaries to the commentaries, and the teachers of the Monastic Rules to the rules. These offerings are made once a year, each on its appointed day. Followers of the Mahayana School make their offerings to Saint Prajna-paramita, Manjusri and Avalokitesvara.

When the monks have received their yearly offerings, the elders, laymen Brahmans, and others bring all manner of robes and necessities to offer to them. And the monks also make offerings to one another. These rituals and rules of conduct for holy monks have been handed down without interruption since Buddha's Nirvana.

After passing the Indus River, proceeding towards Southern India, it is forty to fifty thousand *li* to the sea in the south. And all this land is flat, without great mountains or valleys, having only rivers and streams.

21. The Country of Samkasya

Eighteen *yojanas* towards the southeast there is a country called Samkasya, where Buddha descended from the Trayastrimsas Heaven* after ascending to preach the Law to his mother for three months. Buddha went up to heaven by the exercise of supernatural power, unknown to his disciples. Before the elapse of seven days, through his miraculous power he flew,

---

*The thirty-third heaven.

and thus Aniruddha with his divine sight saw the Blessed One afar off.

"You may go to salute the Blessed One," said Aniruddha to the Venerable Maudgalaputra.

Accordingly Maudgalaputra went to worship at Buddha's feet and exchanged greetings with him.

This done, Buddha said to him, "After seven days I shall descend to Jambudvipa."

Then Maudgalaputra returned to earth.

At this time, the great kings, ministers and people of the eight countries round were all eager to see Buddha, having been deprived of the sight of him for so long, and they assembled like clouds to wait for the Blessed One.

Then a nun by the name of Utpala thought: "Now the kings, ministers and people have all come here to meet Buddha. I am only a woman — how can I see him first?"

Thereupon, by means of supernatural power, she transformed herself into a holy, universal monarch,* and as such she was the very first to render homage to Buddha.

When Buddha descended from the Trayastrimsas Heaven, three gem-studded ladders appeared in the air, and Buddha walked down the ladder in the centre, which was made of the seven precious substances. The god Brahma caused a white silver ladder to appear at

---

*The Wheel King, Chakravartti Raja or universal monarch, ruled over one continent or more.

the right side, and on this, holding a white duster in his hand, he attended Buddha. The god Sakra caused a bright gold ladder to appear at the left side, on which, holding a parasol made of the seven precious substances, he attended Buddha. Countless devas followed Buddha to earth. When Buddha had come down, all three ladders disappeared into the ground, only seven steps remaining visible. Afterwards King Asoka,* wishing to know how deep into the ground the ladders had penetrated, sent men to dig down and find out. They went on digging till they reached the Yellow Spring at the base of the earth, yet still did not reach the bottom. This increased the king's faith and reverence, and he built a temple over the steps. On the central step he placed a full-length statue of Buddha sixteen feet high. Behind the temple he erected a stone pillar thirty cubits high, on the top of which he placed the figure of a lion. On the four sides of the pillar, which was clear and transparent as glass, images of Buddha were carved.

Once a heretical teacher came to the monks and contested their right to live here.

Defeated in argument, the monks prayed together: "If this is where we should live, let there be some miracle to prove it!"

As they uttered this prayer, the lion on top of the pillar gave a loud roar as a sign. Then the heretic was frightened and, humbled, went away.

---

*A famous Indian monarch of the third century B.C.

After living on heavenly food for three months, Buddha's body emitted a heavenly fragrance, very different from that of men. So at once he took a bath, and a bathhouse was built here by men of later years, the same which is there today. A stupa was also built at the spot where the nun Utpala was the first to worship Buddha. There are also stupas at the places where Buddha cut his hair and pared his nails, as well as where the three former Buddhas and Sakyamuni Buddha* sat or walked, and wherever there were images or traces of the Buddhas. These stupas still remain. A stupa was also built where Lord Sakra and the god Brahma came down to earth with Buddha. Here are about a thousand monks and nuns, who take their meals together and study both Mahayana and Hinayana Buddhism. At their dwelling place is a white-eared dragon that acts as their patron. It brings this region rich harvests and rain in season and preserves it from all misfortunes, so that the monks may live in security. The monks, grateful for its favours, have built a house for the dragon and provided it with a seat. Moreover, sacrificial food is prepared and offered to it, and every day three monks are selected to take their meal in the dragon's house. At

---

*Buddhists believe that a Buddha appears from time to time in the world to preach the true doctrine. After a certain lapse of time this teaching is corrupted and lost, and is not restored till a new Buddha appears. In Europe, Buddha is used to designate Sakyamuni (Gautama) Buddha. The three former Buddhas referred to here were Krakuchchanda, Kanakamuni and Kasyapa.

the end of each summer retirement, the dragon often assumes the form of a little serpent whose ears are edged with white. The monks, recognizing it, place it in a copper vessel filled with curds, and carry it around from the highest seat to the lowest as if to pay greetings to all. After making the rounds it disappears. It comes out once every year.

This country is rich and fertile, with a people prosperous and happy beyond compare. The men of other lands, coming here, are entertained and provided with all they need.

22. The Temple of Agnidagdha

Fifty *yojanas* north of this monastery is a temple called Agnidagdha. Agnidagdha was formerly an evil spirit, whom Buddha converted. After this conversion, people built a temple at this spot and offered it to the Arhat. Once, when the Arhat washed his hands here, some drops of water fell on the ground, the traces of which are still apparent. In spite of constant sweeping, they have never disappeared.

Here there is another stupa for Buddha, which is always swept and kept clean by good spirits without the help of men.

"Since you spirits have this ability," said a heretical king, "I shall station a large body of troops here, who will pile up dirt and filth. Will you be able to clear all that away?"

41

But the spirits caused a great wind to spring up, which blew the place clean.

There are a hundred small stupas here, but no one can count the actual number even if he spends a whole day trying. If he insists on knowing the number, he can place a man by the side of each stupa and then count the men. But still there will sometimes be more and sometimes less, and it will be impossible to tell the number exactly.

There is another monastery here where six to seven hundred monks live. This is where a Pratyeka Buddha once fed, and here is the place—about the size of a cart-wheel—where he entered Nirvana. Grass grows all around, but not on that spot; neither does it grow on the place where he sunned his clothes. The marks made by the stripes on his clothes can still be seen on the ground.

23. The City of Kanyakubja and the Village of Hari

Fa-hsien stayed in the Dragon's House for the summer retirement, and when summer was over travelled seven *yojanas* towards the southeast, to the city of Kanyakubja. This city is on the Ganges and has two monasteries, both belonging to the Hinayana School. Six or seven *li* to the west of the city, on the northern bank of the Ganges, is a place where Buddha expounded the Law to his disciples. Tradition has it that here he discoursed upon impermanence and pain, the likeness of the body to a bubble or foam, and other similar matters. A stupa was built there which remains to this day.

Crossing the Ganges and continuing three *yojanas* towards the south, they reached a village called Hari, in which stupas were built at the places where Buddha preached the Law, where he walked and where he sat.

24. The Great Country of Vaisakha

Going southeast for ten *yojanas,* they reached the great country of Vaisakha. Outside the South Gate of the city of Vaisakha and on the east side of the road is the place where Buddha planted a willow twig which he had used to clean his teeth with. This willow grew to exactly seven feet, and thereafter never increased or diminished. Excited by envy and jealousy, heretical Brahmans would often cut it down or uproot it and throw it far away; but another willow always sprang up in the same place as before. Here too they built stupas where the four Buddhas walked and sat. The ruins are there to this day.

25. The City of Sravasti in the Country of Kosala and the Jetavana Retreat

Travelling northward for eight *yojanas,* they reached the city of Sravasti in the country of Kosala. This city is sparsely populated, having only about two hundred families in it. It was under the rule of King Prasenajit. Stupas were later built in this city on the sites of the ruined monastery of Mahaprajapati and the home of the elder Sudatta, and over the spots where Angulimalya attained sainthood and was cremated after he entered Nirvana. Out of jealousy, heretical Brahmans planned to destroy these stupas; but the heavens thundered and lightning flashed so that they were foiled.

About 1,200 paces out of the South Gate of this city and on the west side of the road is a temple built by the elder Sudatta. Its door faces east and it has two chambers before which stand two stone pillars. On the top of the left pillar is the image of a wheel, and on top of the right one the image of an ox. The water in the pool is clear, the trees and plants luxuriant, and flowers of many colours make a lovely sight. This place is called the Jetavana Retreat.

When Buddha ascended the Trayastrimsas Heaven to preach the Law to his mother for ninety days, King Prasenajit, eager to see his face, carved an image of him out of *gosirsha* sandalwood and placed it on the seat on which Buddha usually sat. When Buddha returned to the retreat, the image left its seat and went out to meet him.

"You may keep that seat," said Buddha. "After my Nirvana you will be the model from which my followers of the four groups* will make images."

---

*I.e. monks, nuns, laymen and lay-women.

Upon hearing this, the image returned to its seat. This was the first image ever made of Buddha, and later generations copied it.

Then Buddha moved to a smaller dwelling on the south, about twenty paces from the one occupied by this image.

The Jetavana Retreat originally had seven storeys. And the rulers and citizens of many countries vied with one another in making offerings here, hanging silk pennants and canopies, scattering flowers and lighting lamps which burnt day and night without ever being extinguished. Then a rat carried off the wick from one lamp in its mouth, thereby setting fire to the flowers, pennants and canopies. The whole seven-storey building went up in flames. The rulers and citizens of all the countries round lamented bitterly, thinking that the sandalwood image must also have been burnt. But four or five days later, when they opened the door of the small dwelling on the east, they were amazed and overjoyed to find the image unscathed. Together they rebuilt the retreat as a two-storey building, and moved the image back to its original place.

On arriving at the Jetavana Retreat, when Fa-hsien and Tao-chen reflected that the Blessed One had lived here for twenty-five years, they regretted having been born in a far-off country. Of the companions who had travelled with them through many lands, some had returned to their homes and some had died. As they gazed at the places where Buddha could no longer be seen, they were deeply moved and their hearts were filled with sorrow.

The monks there came forward to question them. "Where do you come from?" they asked.

"We come from China," replied Fa-hsien and Tao-chen.

"How wonderful," exclaimed the monks, "that men from a far-off country should come all this way to seek for the Law!" And they commented to each other: "Not from the earliest times has any of our teachers ever seen a Chinese monk here!"

Four *li* to the northwest of this retreat is a wood named "Sight Restored." There had been five hundred blind men living near this retreat, but when Buddha preached to them they all recovered their sight and were so overjoyed that they drove their staffs into the ground and prostrated themselves to pay homage to Buddha. The staffs took root in the earth and grew into trees, and out of respect no one ventured to cut them down. Thus the place became a wood, and was named the Wood of Sight Restored. Here the monks of the Jetavana Retreat often go after their mid-day meal to sit in meditation.

Six or seven *li* northeast of the Jetavana Retreat is the site of the monastery Mother Vaisakha built for Buddha and his monks. The ruins can still be seen.

The spacious grounds of the Jetavana Retreat have two gates, one facing east and the other north. It was in this garden that the elder Sudatta covered the ground with gold coins to buy the site for Buddha. The retreat is at the centre of the garden, and Buddha spent longer here than in any other place. Stupas, each with a distinctive name, have been built where he preached for the salvation of men, and where he walked and sat. Here too is the spot where the courtesan Sundari was murdered in order to slander Buddha.*

Seventy paces north of the east gate of Jetavana Garden, on the west of the road is the place where Buddha debated with the followers of ninety-six heretical sects. The king, his ministers and the lay Buddhists all gathered to hear the disputation. An envious woman heretic named Chinchimana fastened a bundle of clothes to her belly to make it appear as if she were with child. Then before the whole assembly she accused Buddha of evil conduct. On seeing this, the king of the gods, Sakra, transformed himself into a white mouse and nibbled through her sash so that the bundle fell to the ground. The earth gaped, and she fell alive into hell. Here too is the spot where Devadatta, who poisoned his nails in order to murder Buddha, also fell alive into hell. All these places were marked by later generations. At the spot

---

*Some heretics sent Sundari regularly to listen to Buddha preaching. Later they murdered her and buried her corpse in Jetavana Garden, and then announced that Buddha had killed her to conceal his illicit relationship with her.

where the disputation with the heretics took place, a shrine about sixty feet high was also built, containing an image of Buddha seated.

On the east of the road is a temple named "Overshadowed." This is also about sixty feet in height and was built by Brahman heretics just opposite the shrine erected over the debating place. This temple is so named because, when the sun is in the west, the shadow of the Buddhist shrine covers the heretics' temple; but when the sun is in the east, the shadow of the heretics' temple falls towards the north and can never overshadow the Buddhist shrine.

The heretics sent men regularly to look after their temple, sweep it, water it, burn incense, light the lamps and present offerings. But by the morning their lamps always disappeared, and they would discover them in the Buddhist shrine. The Brahmans grew angry, and said, "The monks are taking our lamps to offer to Buddha. We must stop them." So they kept a watch by night. Then they saw the gods they worshipped take the lamps, circle the Buddhist shrine three times, offer the lamps before the image of Buddha, then suddenly disappear. At that the Brahmans realized that Buddha was greater than their gods, and they forsook their homes to become his followers. It was said that this had occurred only recently.

Around the Jetavana Retreat are ninety-eight monasteries, of which all but one are occupied by monks.

In the Middle Kingdom there are ninety-six heretical sects, who claim to know not only the present but the future. Each sect has its disciples, who also ask for alms but do not use alms-bowls. They also do good deeds, building hospices by the side of solitary roads to provide shelter, bedding, food and drink for wayfarers, monks and passers-by. But their aim in doing this is not like that of the Buddhists.*

Here are also Devadatta's disciples, who make offerings to the three former Buddhas but not to Sakyamuni Buddha.

Four *li* southeast of the city of Sravasti is the place where Buddha stood by the roadside when King Virudhaka set out to attack the Sakya clan. A stupa has been built to mark the spot.

Fifty *li* to the west of this city, they reached a town called Tadwa, where Kasyapa Buddha was born, where he met his father and where he entered Nirvana. Stupas have been built at all these places. A large stupa has also been built over the remains of Kasyapa Buddha.

26. The Town of Napika, the City of Kapilavastu and the Garden of Lumbini

Travelling twelve *yojanas* southeast from the city of Sravasti, they arrived at a town called Napika, where Krakuchchanda Buddha was born, met his father and

---

*Buddhists consider the performance of good deeds a means to attain final emancipation, whereas these heretics did good in order to be rewarded with happiness on earth or in heaven.

entered Nirvàna. Monasteries and stupas have been built at these places.

Less than one *yojana* to the north they reached the town where Kanakamuni Buddha was born, met his father and entered Nirvana. Stupas have been built at all these places.

Less than one *yojana* to the east they reached the city of Kapilavastu. This city has neither king nor citizens, and looks completely deserted; for here live only some monks and a few dozen families of the laity. Among the ruins of the palace of King Suddhodana is an image of the prince's mother, showing the prince,* riding on a white elephant, coming to enter his mother's womb. A stupa has been built over the spot where the prince, having left the city by the East Gate, saw a sick man and ordered his charioteer to drive back to the palace. Here too are the places where Asita observed the marks on the prince, and where the prince with Ananda and others brought down an elephant. An arrow shot from here entered the earth thirty *li* to the southeast, causing a fountain to spring up; and the people made a well from which wayfarers might drink. Stupas have also been built at the following places: where Buddha returned to see his father after attaining Buddha-hood; where the earth quaked six times when five hundred men of the Sakya clan saluted Upali after renouncing their homes; where Buddha expounded the Law to devas while the four celestial kings guarded the four

_____

*I.e. Buddha.

gates of the hall so that his father, the king, could not enter; and where Buddha sat facing east under a *nyagrodha* tree — which is growing to this day — while Mahaprajapati offered him a robe. Here also can be found the stupa built at the place where King Virudhaka slaughtered the descendants of the Sakya clan, who had all attained to the first stage of sainthood. A few *li* to the northeast of the city is the royal field where the prince sat under a tree to watch men ploughing. Fifty *li* to the east of the city is the royal garden called Lumbini. It was in this garden that the queen entered the pond to bathe. After bathing she came out from the northern side of the pond, walked for about twenty paces and, holding the branch of a tree and facing east, gave birth to a princely son. As soon as the prince was born he took seven steps, and was bathed by two dragon-kings. A well has been made at that bathing place, and monks often drink the water from it as well as from the pond.

Four places are always determined in advance: where Buddhas shall attain Buddha-hood; where they shall begin to preach; where they shall expound the Law and refute heretics; and where they shall descend from the Trayastrimsas Heaven after having preached to their mothers. Other places are chosen according to circumstances.

The country of Kapilavastu is deserted and few people travel its roads for fear of the white elephants and lions there. One cannot journey without taking great precautions.

51

27. The Country of Ramagrama

Five *yojanas* east of Buddha's birthplace lies the
country of Ramagrama. The king of this country
obtained a share of the relics of Buddha, and upon his
return home built a stupa named Ramagrama. Beside
this stupa is a pond in which lives a dragon that
keeps constant guard over the stupa and worships there
day and night. When King Asoka was living, he determined to demolish eight stupas and built 84,000 new
ones; and having pulled down seven, he came to raze
this of Ramagrama. But then the dragon appeared
and took him to its palace, where it showed him all the
vessels it used in worship.

"If your vessels are better than mine," it said to the
king, "then destroy this stupa and take it away, and I
will not quarrel with you."

Knowing that the dragon's vessels were not of this
world, King Asoka had to go home.

Since this place was completely deserted, there was
no one to sweep and water it. But a herd of elephants
would often come with water in their trunks to water
the ground, and they offered fragrant blossoms of many
kinds here. A monk who came from another country
to worship at this stupa was terrified at the sight of
the elephants, and hid behind a tree. But when he saw
these beasts presenting offerings in the approved manner, he was deeply moved to think that there were no
monks here to look after this stupa and that it was left
to the elephants to keep it clean. He thereupon gave

up his status as a fully ordained monk to take up the duties of a novice,* cutting the weeds and brambles himself and levelling the ground, till all was in good order. This done, he urged the king to build a monastery there, and volunteered to be the abbot of it. There are monks now living there. This occurred recently, and the abbot of this monastery has always been a novice since that time.

Three *yojanas* east of this is the place where the prince dismissed Chandaka and his white horse. A stupa has also been built here.

Travelling east again for four *yojanas*, they arrived at the Ashes Stupa, where there is also a monastery.

28. The City of Kusinagara

Twelve *yojanas* further east, they reached the city of Kusinagara. It was north of this city, between two trees beside the Hiranyavati River, that Buddha entered Nirvana with his head towards the north. Here are stupas and monasteries which were built at the following places: where Subhadra, Buddha's last disciple, entered the Order; where the Blessed One, lying in a golden coffin, received homage for seven days; where Vajrapani laid down his golden

---

*A fully ordained Buddhist monk is not supposed to perform certain manual labour, such as digging or cutting grass; but a novice, or *sramanera*, is allowed to do such things.

mace; and where the eight kings shared the relics of Buddha. This city is almost deserted, with only a handful of monks and a few laymen as its inhabitants.

29. The Last Farewell of the Lichchhavis to Buddha

Travelling twelve *yojanas* to the southeast they reached the spot where the Lichchhavis wished to follow Buddha to the place of his Nirvana, but could not gain his consent. Out of affection for him they would not go away; so Buddha made a deep ditch appear which they were unable to cross. He then gave them his alms-bowl as a relic, and sent them home. A stone pillar with inscriptions was erected at this place.

30. The Country of Vaisali, the Stupa of Bows and Lances Laid Down, and the Council for Collating the Monastic Rules

Continuing five *yojanas* to the east, they arrived at the country of Vaisali. North of the city of Vaisali is the storeyed Monastery of the Great Forest in which Buddha lived and the stupa built for half the relics of Ananda. In this city also dwelt the Lady Amrapali, who built a stupa for Buddha, the ruins of which may still be seen today.

West of the road three *li* to the south of the city is the garden which the Lady Amrapali offered to Buddha as a dwelling place.

When Buddha was approaching the time of his Nirvana, he left Vaisali with his disciples by the West Gate and, turning to his right, looked back at the city and said: "This is the last place I shall have visited." Later a stupa was built on that spot.

Three *li* northwest of the city is the Stupa of Bows and Lances Laid Down, which received this name because of the following happenings:

In the upper reaches of the Ganges lived a king, one of whose inferior wives gave birth to an unformed foetus. The queen, who was jealous, said: "You have given birth to an omen of misfortune."

Then they put the foetus in a chest, and threw it into the Ganges.

Another king, who was then on a pleasure trip in the lower reaches of the Ganges, saw the chest floating in the river. Having brought it ashore and opened it, he found it contained a thousand handsome, royal-looking infants. The king brought them up and they grew into brave, strong warriors, who conquered every country they attacked. And at last they came to attack their father's kingdom. The king was so greatly dismayed that his inferior wife asked what had caused him such alarm.

"The king of a neighbouring state has a thousand sons," he told her. "They are all of them brave and strong beyond compare, and now they are coming to attack us. That is why I am alarmed."

"Do not let that alarm you, O King," she said. "If you build a high pavilion on the east of the city and place me on it when the invaders come, I shall be able to quell them."

The king did as she proposed. And when the invaders came the inferior wife called to them from the top of the pavilion.

"You are all my sons," she cried. "What makes you so rebellious?"

"Who are you that claim to be our mother?" they asked.

"If you do not believe me," she said, "look up, and open your mouths."

Then she pressed her breasts with both hands, and from each breast gushed five hundred jets of milk, which spurted into the mouths of her thousand sons. Thereupon the invaders realized that she was indeed their mother, and laid down their bows and lances.

Meditating on this event, both the kings became Pratyeka Buddhas. The two stupas built in their honour are standing today.

After his accession to Buddha-hood, Buddha informed his disciples: "This is where I laid down my bow and lance."

When the people knew this, they built a stupa there, and gave it this name.

The thousand sons were in fact the thousand Buddhas of this *Bhadra-kalpa*.*

By the side of the Stupa of Bows and Lances Laid Down, Buddha said to Ananda: "After another three months I shall enter Nirvana."

But Ananda was so bewitched by the king of demons at the time that he did not request Buddha to remain longer in the world.

Three or four *li* to the east of this there stands another stupa. One hundred years after Buddha's Nirvana, some monks in Vaisali began to commit ten acts forbidden by the Law, and defended themselves by maintaining that Buddha had decreed these practices. Then the Arhats, monks, and laymen—seven hundred in all—who strictly observed the rules, edited and collated the Monastic Rules afresh. And a stupa was later built here, which remains to this day.

31. The Confluence of the Five Rivers and the Death of Ananda

From here they journeyed eastward for four *yojanas* till they came to the confluence of the five rivers. When Ananda was travelling from Magadha to Vaisali, intending to enter Nirvana there, the devas informed King Ajatasatru of it. Then the king, at the head of his troops, hastened to the bank of the river. And

----

*A *kalpa* is a period of time. *Bhadra-kalpa* is the present cosmic age.

the Lichchhavis of Vaisali also, hearing that Ananda
was coming, came to meet him on the opposite bank.
Ananda reflected that if he proceeded King Ajatasatru
would be grieved, while if he turned back the Lichchhavis would complain. Accordingly he went to the
middle of the river where he engaged in the Fire
Meditation and by this means burnt himself to death.
His remains were divided into two portions, one for
each side of the river. Thus each of the kings had
half of Ananda's relics, and they built stupas for them
after returning home.

32. The City of Pataliputra in the Country of Magadha

After crossing the river and travelling one *yojana*
south, they reached the city of Pataliputra in the country of Magadha. Pataliputra was King Asoka's capital.
The royal palaces in the city were all constructed by
genii and spirits. The walls and arches are of stone,
with carvings and sculptures cut by no human hand.
The ruins can still be seen.

The younger brother of King Asoka, having attained
Arhatship, spent all his time on Gridhrakuta Mountain,
where he found pleasure in quietness and repose. To
show his respect, the king invited him to his palace.
But since the recluse enjoyed living in the quiet hills,
he declined the invitation.

"If you will consent to come," said the king, "I shall
make a hill inside the city for you."

Then the king prepared food and drink and summoned genii and spirits.

"I hope you will all accept my invitation for tomorrow," he said. "But as there are no seats, I must request each of you to bring your own."

On the following day each of the great genii and spirits came with a huge boulder four or five paces square. After the feast was over, the king asked the genii and spirits to pile up these rocks to make a hill, using five boulders to form a cave underneath, about thirty feet in length, twenty in breadth and more than ten feet in height.

There was a Brahman of the Mahayana School named Radhasvami living in this city. Intelligent and wise, he had mastered all the knowledge of his time, and he lived in a state of tranquillity. The king respected him as his religious teacher, and dared not sit in his presence whenever he paid him a call. If the king took his hand out of affection or respect, the Brahman would wash himself afterwards. Almost fifty years old, he was honoured by the whole country. It was due to this one man that Buddhism was propagated and the heretics could gain no advantages over the Buddhists.

By the side of King Asoka's stupa is a magnificent Mahayana monastery. There is also a Hinayana monastery, and in these two monasteries live six or seven hundred monks whose behaviour is most decorous and orderly. Monks of high virtue and scholars from every quarter flock here to seek for knowledge and truth. The Brahman teacher Manjusri, who is honoured by all the holy monks and devout Mahayana priests of the country, also resides in this monastery.

33. The Image Procession and the Charitable Hospital

Pataliputra is the largest city in the whole Middle Kingdom. The people are rich and prosperous, and vie with each other in performing good deeds. Every year in celebration of the eighth day of the second month they hold an image procession. They use a four-wheeled cart on which five tiers are constructed in bamboo, with a halberd-shaped central post about twenty feet high, the whole structure resembling a pagoda. This is covered with white woollen cloth, painted with various devas in colour, adorned with gold, silver and glass, and hung with silk pennants and canopies. There are four shrines on the four sides, each containing a seated Buddha, attended by standing Bodhisattvas. About twenty such cars are prepared, each decked out in a different way. On the day of the procession the monks and laymen of the country assemble to dance, play music and offer flowers and incense. The Brahmans come out to receive the images of Buddha, which are brought into the city one after the other, and remain there till the next day. Lamps burn throughout the night, and there is dancing and music to honour the gods. This ceremony is the same in all the Buddhist countries.

The elders and laymen of this country have established charitable hospitals in the city, to which all the poor, homeless, deformed and ill can go. Here all their wants are supplied, and the physicians who attend them prescribe the food and medicine they require. When cured, they are free to leave.

King Asoka, after he had destroyed seven stupas, built 84,000 new ones, the first being the great stupa three *li* or more to the south of this city. In front of this is one of Buddha's footprints, over which a temple has been erected, its door opening north towards the stupa. South of the stupa there is a stone pillar fourteen or fifteen feet around and more than thirty feet high. The inscription upon this reads:

"King Asoka offered Jambudvipa to monks from all parts of the world, then redeemed it again with silver. And this he did three times."

Three or four hundred paces north of the stupa is the site of the city of Niraya which King Asoka built, and here stands a stone pillar more than thirty feet high, with the figure of a lion above it. An inscription on the pillar relates the reason for building it and the year, the month and the day.

34. The Solitary Crag and the Village of Kalapinaka

Travelling southeast from here for nine *yojanas*, they arrived at a solitary crag. On the summit of the crag is a stone cell, facing south, with a seated image of Buddha in it. This is where Sakra sent the heavenly musician Panchasikha to play the harp for Buddha's pleasure, and it was here also that Sakra questioned Buddha on forty-two points. Buddha traced a line on the rock with his finger at each question, and the marks of his finger are there to this day. There is also a monastery here.

One *yojana* to the southwest, they reached the village of Kalapinaka. This is where Sariputra was born, and here he returned to enter Nirvana. A stupa built here is standing to this day.

35. The New City of Rajagriha and the Old City of King Bimbisara

One *yojana* to the west they arrived at the new city of Rajagriha, built by King Ajatasatru. There are two monasteries here. Three hundred paces out of the West Gate of the city towers the magnificent stupa built by King Ajatasatru over the share of Buddha's relics which he obtained.

Leaving the city by the southern side and proceeding for four *li*, they entered a valley surrounded by five hills as if by a city wall. This is the site of the old city of King Bimbisara, which is five or six *li* from east to west, and seven or eight *li* from north to south. This is where Sariputra and Maudgalaputra first met Asvajit, where Nirgrantha made a fiery pit

62

and prepared poisoned rice for Buddha, and where King Ajatasatru gave wine to a black elephant in order to injure Buddha. In the garden of Ambapali in the northeast corner of this city Jivaka built a monastery to invite Buddha and his 1,250 disciples to receive his offerings. The ruins still remain. But the city is desolate, without inhabitants.

36. Gridhrakuta Mountain

After entering the valley and travelling fifteen *li* to the mountains in the southeast, they reached Gridhrakuta Mountain. Three *li* from the summit of the mountain is a cave facing south, in which Buddha used to sit in meditation. About thirty paces to the northwest is another cave where Ananda was once sitting in meditation when Mara Pisuna took the form of a vulture and hovered in front of the cave to terrify him. But Buddha with his supernatural powers stretched his hand through the rock and patted Ananda's shoulder, so that his fears were allayed. The traces of the vulture and the hole made by Buddha's hand can still be seen today. Thus the name of this mountain is called the Mountain of the Vulture Cave. In front of the cave is the place where the four Buddhas sat. The Arhats each have a cave in which to meditate — several hundred in all. Once Buddha was pacing to and fro in front of his cave when Devadatta rolled down a stone from the precipice in the north, injuring Buddha's toe. The stone is there to this day. The hall in which Buddha preached the Law has been destroyed, and only the foundations of the brick walls remain. The peaks of this mountain are beautiful and imposing, and it is the highest of all the five hills.

Fa-hsien bought incense, flowers and oil for lamps in the new city, and requested two resident monks to guide him to Gridhrakuta Mountain. There he offered the incense and flowers and lit the lamps.

"This is where Buddha used to live," he said, shedding tears of emotion. "And here he expounded the *Surangama Sutra*. Fa-hsien, who was born too late to see Buddha himself, can only gaze at the traces left by him and the places where he lived."

He recited the *Surangama Sutra* in front of the cave and, after spending the night there, returned to the new city.

37. The Ruins in the Old City of King Bimbisara

On the west side of the road about three hundred paces out of the North Gate of the old city stands the Retreat of the Karanda Bamboo Grove, which is kept clean by the monks there. Two or three *li* north of the retreat is a *samasana,* or burial ground.

Three hundred paces west along the southern hill is the Cave of Pippala, where Buddha used to sit in

meditation after his meals. Five or six *li* further west
is the Cave of Saptaparna, on the shady side of the
hill. It was here that the five hundred Arhats made a
compilation of the scriptures after Buddha's Nirvana.
During this work, three high seats were prepared and
adorned in a stately manner. Sariputra took the left
seat and Maudgalaputra the right. Of the five hundred
Arhats one was absent, and great Kasyapa presided
over the assembly while Ananda, who was unable to
enter, stood outside the gate. A stupa built at this
spot remains to this day. Along the hillside are many
caves used by the Arhats for meditation.

Three *li* to the east from the North Gate of the old
city is the Cave of Devadatta. Fifty paces from this
there is a great, square, black rock. Once a monk
paced this rock, meditating on the impermanence, sorrow and vanity of life. Conscious of human impurity,
he loathed his body and drawing his knife longed to
kill himself, but then remembered that the Blessed
One had made a rule forbidding suicide. He reflected,
however, that though this was so, he would only be
killing the Three Mortal Foes,* and so he cut his throat.
When his knife gashed the flesh, he attained to the
stage of Srotapanna; when his throat was half severed,
he realized the sainthood of Anagamin; and when he
had made an end of himself, he achieved Arhatship
and entered Nirvana.

---

*Lust, hatred and ignorance.

38. The City of Gaya

Travelling west from here for four *yojanas,* they reached the city of Gaya. This city is desolate and completely deserted.

Going another twenty *li* south, they arrived at the place where Buddha lived as an ascetic for six years. This district is richly wooded.

Three *li* to the west, they visited the spot where Buddha bathed once and a deva lowered the branch of a tree so as to help him out of the water.

Two *li* to the north, they reached the place where the maidens of Gramika offered milk and rice to Buddha.

Two *li* further north is the spot where Buddha sat facing east on a rock under a great tree to eat the rice. Both the tree and the rock are still there. The rock is about six feet square and two feet high. As the climate in the Middle Kingdom is temperate, a tree may grow for several thousand or even ten thousand years.

From here they proceeded northeast for half a *yojana,* till they came to the cave which Buddha entered and in which he sat cross-legged facing the west. He reflected that if he were going to attain to Buddhahood, there should be some divine manifestation. Then the shadow of a Buddha about three feet high — which is still distinctly visible — appeared on the rock wall. At the same time heaven and earth quaked, and devas in the air proclaimed:

"This is not the place for Buddhas of the past or the future to attain to Buddha-hood. In the southwest, under a *pattra* tree less than half a *yojana* from here, is the place for Buddhas of the past and the future to attain to Buddha-hood!"

This said, the devas led the way forward, singing, and Buddha rose and followed them. Thirty paces from the tree, the devas presented him with *kusa* grass, which he accepted. When he had advanced another fifteen paces, five hundred blue birds came flying towards him, encircled him three times and flew away. Having reached the *pattra* tree, he spread the *kusa* grass on the ground and sat down facing the east. Then Mara the demon king sent three beautiful girls from the north to tempt him, and led troops from the south to try him. But Buddha pressed his toe on the ground, and Mara's soldiers retreated in confusion while the three girls turned into old women.

At all these places visited by Buddha while he lived as an ascetic for six years, and at each spot subsequently mentioned, men of later times have built stupas and set up images of Buddha, which exist to this very day. Stupas have also been built at the following places: where Buddha, seven days after his accession to Buddha-hood, looked at the tree and enjoyed the bliss of emancipation; where he walked from east to west for seven days under the *pattra* tree; where the devas raised a terrace of the seven precious substances to make offerings to Buddha for seven days; where the blind dragon Muchilinda revolved around Buddha for seven days; where Buddha sat on a square rock facing east under a *nyagrodha* tree when Brahma came to invite him; where the four celestial kings presented him with his alms-bowl; where the five hundred merchants offered him flour and honey; and where he converted the Kasyapa brothers and their thousand disciples.

There are three monasteries at the place where Buddha attained to Buddha-hood, all of which are occupied by monks. These monks are supported by the local people who supply them liberally with all they need, so that they lack for nothing. The Monastic Rules are strictly kept, and they also observe with decorum the ritual of sitting, rising and taking part in assemblies practised by the holy monks during Buddha's lifetime.

Good care has been taken of the four great stupas ever since Buddha's Nirvana. The four great stupas stand at the place where Buddha was born, where he attained Buddha-hood, where he began to preach, and where he entered Nirvana.

39. The Hell of King Asoka

When King Asoka was a child in a former life, while playing on the road he met Sakyamuni Buddha begging for alms. Delighted, he offered Buddha a handful of earth, which Buddha took to spread on the ground where he used to walk. As a result of this good deed, the child became King of the Iron Wheel and ruled over Jambudvipa. Once, while making a tour of inspection in Jambudvipa, he saw the hell between two iron-encircled hills where the wicked are punished.

"What place is that?" he asked his ministers.

"That is where Yama, the king of spirits, punishes the wicked," they told him.

On hearing this, Asoka reflected that if the king of spirits could make a hell to punish the wicked, why should not he, a ruler of men, make a place of punishment for criminals?

So he asked his ministers: "Who can make a hell for me and take charge of punishing evil-doers there?"

"Only the most wicked man can do that," they replied.

Thereupon the king sent his ministers out in all directions to look for wicked men. Eventually they found a man by the side of a pond who was tall, strong and swarthy, with yellow hair and blue eyes. He could catch fish with his feet, and make birds and beasts come when he called; but then he shot them, not sparing a single one. Having found this man, they sent him to the king.

"Make a square enclosure with high walls," the king charged him secretly. "Plant it with a profusion of flowers and fruit trees and build a handsomely ornamented bathing pool, so that passers-by will be eager to look inside. Make the doors and windows strong. Whenever anyone enters, put him to every torture you can devise and do not let him out again. Even if I should enter the place myself, you must torture me as well, and never let me go. Now I appoint you the keeper of this hell."

Once a monk who was begging from door to door entered the gate of this hell, and the keeper promptly seized him and prepared to torture him. But the terrified monk pleaded with him and was granted a brief respite to have his mid-day meal. At that moment another man came in, and the keeper immediately put him into a mortar and pounded him till a red froth appeared. Having witnessed this, the monk reflected on the impermanence, sorrow and vanity of bodily existence, which is like a bubble or foam upon the water. And so he achieved Arhatship. Thus when the keeper seized and thrust him into a cauldron of boiling water, the monk was glad at heart and his face was serene. The fire went out, the water cooled, and up sprang a lotus flower with the monk sitting upon it.

The keeper went to inform the king of this.

"Something amazing has happened in hell," he said. "Will Your Majesty please go and have a look?"

"I dare not," replied Asoka. "Remember our former agreement."

"This is no small matter, sire," protested the keeper. "Never mind that agreement, but come with me at once."

So the king followed him to the hell. Then the monk expounded the Law to King Asoka, who accepted the faith, destroyed this hell and repented of all the crimes he had committed. From that time on he believed in and respected the Three Precious Gems, and often repaired to a *pattra* tree under which he repented his sins and observed the Eight Precepts.*

"Where is it the king always goes?" inquired the queen.

"His Majesty often goes to the *pattra* tree," replied the ministers.

Then the queen sent someone to fell the tree when Asoka was not there. When he came and saw what had happened, he fell senseless to the ground. His ministers dashed water in his face and eventually he recovered consciousness. He piled up bricks round the stump of the tree and watered its root with a hundred pitchers of milk, then prostrated himself on the ground and vowed:

"If the tree does not grow, I shall never rise again!"

As he uttered this vow the tree began to grow till it reached its present height, which is nearly a hundred feet.

40. The Kukkutapada Mountain

Continuing three *li* to the south, they reached the mountain called Kukkutapada. Kasyapa is at present

---

*Not to kill, not to steal, not to have sexual intercourse, not to tell lies, not to drink wine, nôt to use cosmetics and personal adornments, or to dance and play music, not to sleep on fine beds, and not to take food in the afternoon.

in this mountain. He split the mountain to enter it, but that opening is now closed. And his body is preserved entire in a chasm at a great distance from this in one side of the mountain. Outside the chasm is the place where he washed. his hands. If the people of this country suffer from headaches, they rub the earth from this spot on their heads and the pain is cured. Since Kasyapa's Nirvana Arhats have lived in this mountain, and each year the monks of neighbouring states go there to worship Kasyapa. If anyone comes with doubts in his mind, some Arhat will appear to reason with him by night, disappearing as soon as his doubts have been resolved. This mountain is thickly overgrown with brambles, and is so infested with lions, tigers and wolves, that one cannot wander there freely.

41. The City of Varanasi and the Deer Park

Fa-hsien returned to Pataliputra and, travelling west along the Ganges for ten *yojanas*, arrived at a monastery called Atavi in which Buddha once lived. There are monks in residence now.

Again proceeding west along the Ganges for twelve *yojanas*, he reached the city of Varanasi in the country of Kasi. About ten *li* northeast of the city is the Deer Park Retreat of the Rishis. Originally a Pratyeka Buddha lived in this park, and wild deer often came here for shelter. When the Blessed One was about to become a Buddha, devas announced from the sky:

"The son of King Suddhodana, who renounced his home to acquire supreme truth, will attain to Buddhahood after seven days."

On hearing this, the Pratyeka Buddha entered Nirvana. Therefore his place is called the Deer Park of the Rishis. After the Blessed One's accession to Buddha-hood, men of later ages built a retreat here. Buddha wished to convert Kaundinya and his four companions, but these five men said to each other:

"For six years this monk Gautama lived as an ascetic on one grain of sesame and one of rice a day, yet he did not obtain the truth. Now that he is living among men, having thrown off all mental and physical restraints, what truth can he have obtained? If he comes today, let us be sure not to speak to him."

When Buddha arrived, however, the five men felt impelled to rise and salute him.

Sixty paces further north is the place where Buddha sat facing east when he preached his first sermon and converted Kaundinya and his companions. Twenty paces north of this is the place where Buddha predicted the future of Maitreya. Fifty paces to the south is the spot where the dragon Elapatra asked Buddha when he could be freed from his dragon form. Stupas built at all these spots are standing to this day. There are also two monasteries, both of which are occupied by monks.

42. The Country of Kausambi and the Garden of Ghoshira

Thirteen *yojanas* northwest of the Deer Park Retreat is the country of Kausambi. The monastery there is called the Garden of Ghoshira, and here Buddha once lived. Most of the monks in residence at present study Hinayana Buddhism.

Eight *yojanas* to the east is the spot where Buddha converted an evil demon. Stupas also mark where he lived, walked and sat. A hundred monks or more live in the monastery here.

43. The Country of Dakshina and the Paravati Monastery

Proceeding south for two hundred *yojanas*, they came to the country called Dakshina. Here is a monastery of the former Kasyapa Buddha, hewn out of a great mountain of rock. It has five tiers: the first in the shape of an elephant, with five hundred chambers; the second in the shape of a lion, with four hundred chambers; the third in the shape of a horse, with three hundred chambers; the fourth in the shape of an ox, with two hundred chambers; and the fifth in the shape of a dove, with one hundred chambers. At the very top there is a spring of water which flows down in front of the chambers through a circuitous channel till it reaches the lowest tier, then, passing the chambers, issues at last through the door. A window has been hewn in the rock of every chamber in each tier; thus they receive ample light and no corner is dark. At the four corners of this edifice steps have been hewn in the rock. Since men of the present time are short, they have difficulty in climbing these steps which the men of old ascended easily. This monastery's name is Paravati, which means "dove." There have always been Arhats here. The land is barren and void of inhabitants.

At a great distance from the hill is a village in which all the inhabitants are monks or Brahmans who hold heretical views and do not believe in Buddhism, or are followers of other heretical schools.

The people of this country often see men flying to the monastery here. Thus they ask those monks who come from abroad to worship here:

"Why don't you fly? All the monks we see here can fly."

The monks then answer evasively: "Our wings have not yet grown!"

The roads in Dakshina are dangerous and hard to travel. Even those who hear of the place and wish to go there have to present money or goods to the king of the country, who then appoints men as their guides who will pass them on from one post to another in order to show them the way. Fa-hsien was unable to go there. He has related simply what men of that country told him.

44. The Sanskrit Scriptures and the Sanskrit Language

Travelling east from Benares they returned to Pataliputra. Fa-hsien had come to seek the books of monastic discipline, but in the countries of North India these rules are handed down by word of mouth, hence there were no written records for him to copy. He had therefore to travel as far as Central India, where in a Mahayana monastery he obtained a collection of the precepts of monastic discipline. It was the *Rules of the Mahasanghika,* which was first observed by the great assembly of monks while Buddha was yet alive. This copy has been handed down in the Jetavana Retreat. Though each of the eighteen sects has its own rules of conduct, they agree in all essentials, simply paying more or less attention to certain minor matters. But this book is the most comprehensive. He also obtained a copy of the rules in about 7,000 verses. This was the *Rules of the Sarvastivadah*—the same rules as those observed by monks in China — which was also handed down orally from teacher to pupil without being committed to writing. In this monastery he also obtained a copy of the *Samyuktabhidharma-hridaya Sastra* in about 6,000 verses, a copy of the *Nirvana Sutra* in 2,500 verses, a copy of the *Vaipulya-parinirvana Sutra* in about 5,000 verses, and a copy of the *Commentaries of the Mahasanghika.*

Fa-hsien spent three years in studying written and spoken Sanskrit and in copying these books.

Upon arriving at the Middle Kingdom and seeing the excellent rules and decorous conduct of the monks here in their daily life, Tao-chen sighed over the imperfect rules of the monks in far-away China and prayed that never again might he be reborn in a far-off country till he should attain to Buddha-hood. So he settled down in India and never returned to China. But Fa-hsien had gone there in order to bring back the Monastic Rules to China, so he returned, alone.

45. The Great Country of Champa and the Kingdom of Tamralipti

Eighteen *yojanas* to the east along the Ganges, on the south bank of the river, is the great country of Champa. Stupas have been built at Buddha's dwelling place, where he walked and where the four Buddhas sat. There are monks living there.

Nearly fifty *yojanas* to the east, Fa-hsien reached Tamralipti which borders on the sea. Here there are twenty-four monasteries, all with monks living in them, and Buddhism flourishes. After staying here for two years to copy sutras and make drawings of Buddha's images, he set sail in a large merchant ship across the ocean towards the southwest. Taking advantage of the fair wind of early winter, the vessel sailed for fourteen days and nights till it reached Simhala, the Country of the Lion.

46. Simhala, the Country of the Lion

The people of Simhala informed Fa-hsien that the distance of the voyage was about seven hundred *yojanas*. The Country of the Lion is an island some fifty *yojanas* from east to west and thirty from north to south. To its left and right are about a hundred small islands, ten, twenty or two hundred *li* from each other, all of which are under the rule of this large island. Most of these islands produce precious stones and pearls, and there is a district of about ten square *li* which produces the *mani* jewel. The king has posted guards here, and takes a levy of three-tenths of the jewels that are found.

There were originally no inhabitants here, only spirits and dragons. When merchants from other countries came to trade, the spirits did not appear, but simply set out their rare merchandise with the prices marked. The merchants paid accordingly, and took away the goods directly. Owing to this traffic of merchants, the people of all the countries round heard how pleasant a land this was, and came here too. In this way a large kingdom was formed. The climate is temperate, winter and summer alike. Plants and trees bloom the whole year round, and the fields may be sown whenever the people please — there are no fixed seasons.

47. Buddha's Footprints and the Monastery Called Abhayagiri

Buddha once came to this country to convert a wicked dragon. With his supernatural powers, he planted one foot at the north of the royal city and one on a mountain top fifteen *yojanas* away. Over the footprint north of the royal city, a great stupa four hundred feet high was built, adorned with gold and silver and studded with all kinds of jewels. By the side of this stupa a monastery was erected which is called Abhayagiri (The Hill of Fearlessness), and here are five thousand monks. It contains a hall for the worship of Buddha, engraved with gold and silver and adorned with precious stones. In it stands an image of Buddha made of green jade, some twenty feet high. The entire image sparkles with the seven precious substances, and its splendour and magnificence defy description. In its right hand the image holds a priceless pearl.

Fa-hsien had left China for many years and associated with none but men of foreign lands. All the mountains, rivers, plants and trees that he saw were strange to him. Moreover, his companions had left him — some had remained behind, while some had died. Looking at his lonely shadow, he was often filled with sadness. So when he stood by the side of this jade image and happened to see a white silk fan from China — the offering of some merchant — tears filled his eyes and he gave way to his grief.

A former king of this country had sent a messenger to the Middle Kingdom to fetch a seed of the *pattra* tree to plant beside the hall, and this grew some two hundred feet high. This tree inclined towards the southeast and, fearing that it might fall, the king set up a huge pillar that required eight or nine men to encircle it, to support the tree. At the place where the tree was propped, a branch grew out from the trunk and pierced the pillar, then sent down roots to the ground. This branch was so thick it took four men to encircle it. Though the pillar is cleft in two, since it still supports the tree it has not been removed.

Under this tree is a rest house containing a seated image of Buddha, to which both monks and laymen pay homage continuously. In this city there is also the Temple of Buddha's Tooth, constructed entirely of the seven precious substances. The king leads a pure life and observes the Buddhist precepts, while the citizens of the capital also have the greatest reverence for Buddhism. Since the establishment of this kingdom, there has been no famine or trouble here. The monks' store-houses are filled with precious stones and *mani* jewels. When the king once went to inspect these store-houses and saw the *mani* jewels, he coveted them and longed to seize them. After three days, however, he repented, and going to the monks and saluting them he confessed the evil desire he had felt.

"I hope you will make it a rule," he told the monks, "never to let the king inspect your store-houses; and

admit no monk who has not been in the Order for
forty years."

48. Buddha's Tooth and the
Monastery of Bodhi

In this city are many Buddhist laymen, elders and
merchants of all trades. The houses are beautiful, the
roads level and trim. Preaching-halls have been built
at the crossroads, where, on the eighth, fourteenth and
fifteenth of each month, high seats are set, and monks,
laymen and believers of the four groups gather to
listen to the preaching of the Law. The people of this
country say there are about 60,000 monks fed at the
public expense, while the king supports five or six
thousand more in the royal city. Those who need food
may bring their own alms-bowls to fetch it, and carry
away as much as the vessel contains.

Buddha's tooth is usually displayed in the middle
of the third month. Ten days before this event, the
king adorns and caparisons a great elephant, and bids
an orator in royal robes ride on this elephant and sound
a drum, then make this proclamation:

"For three *Asankhyeya-kalpas*,* Buddha practised
asceticism. Never sparing himself, he gave up his
kingdom, his wife and son, and even tore out his eye
to give to another. He cut his own flesh to deliver
a dove, gave away his head as alms, offered his body

---

*Previous cosmic ages.

to a ravenous tiger, and did not grudge his marrow and brain. Having suffered these pains for the sake of all living creatures, at last he became a Buddha. While in this world he spent forty-nine years expounding the Law and edifying the people. He gave rest to the weary, and saved those who were lost. And when he had fulfilled his mission among men, he entered Nirvana. Since his Nirvana, 1,497 years have passed, during which the Eye of the World has been closed and all living creatures have never ceased to grieve. Ten days from now, Buddha's tooth will be brought out and carried to Abhayagiri Monastery. All monks and laymen who wish to do good deeds may level the road, adorn the lanes and streets, and prepare all kinds of flowers and incense as offerings."

After this proclamation, on both sides of the road the king sets images of the five hundred forms which Buddha assumed in his earlier existence, when, for example, he was born as Sudana, Sama, the king of the elephants, a deer and a horse. Painted and richly adorned, these images appear extremely lifelike. Then Buddha's tooth is brought out and carried along the main road, and offerings are made to it all along the way till it reaches the hall in Abhayagiri Monastery. There monks and laymen gather to burn incense, light lamps and perform all manner of religious ceremonies day and night without rest. After ninety days, the tooth is carried back to the temple in the city. And this temple is open on fast days so that believers may worship the tooth according to the Buddhist custom

Forty *li* to the east of Abhayagiri Monastery there is another hill, and on it stands a monastery called Bodhi, in which live some 2,000 monks. Among them is a monk of great virtue, by the name of Dharmakirti, whom the people of this country revere. He has lived in a stone cell for some forty years. And, such is his compassion, he can make serpents and mice live together without injuring each other.

49. Mahavihara Monastery

Seven *li* to the south of this city is Mahavihara Monastery, where live 3,000 monks. There was once a monk here of the highest virtue, who observed the Monastic Rules so faithfully that the people of the country suspected he must be an Arhat. When he was about to die the king came to visit him and, in accordance with the Buddhist custom, assembled all the monks. Then in their presence he asked this monk: "Have you attained to sainthood?"

At that the other told him the truth: "I am an Arhat."

After his death, the king had him cremated four or five *li* east of the monastery, in accordance with the funeral ceremony for Arhats decreed by the Monastic Rules. A fine, great pyre of wood was built, about thirty feet square and thirty feet high, with sandalwood, aloes and other aromatic wood at its top. Steps were made at the four sides, and the whole pyre was covered with snowy white woollen cloth of the best quality. Above the pyre would be the bier, similar to the hearse which is used in China, except that it had no dragon and fish designs. At the time of the cremation, the king and people, including all the believers of the four groups, assembled together. After offering flowers and incense, they followed the bier to the place of cremation. The king then made his personal offerings of flowers and incense. This done, the bier was placed on top of the pyre, great quantities of butter were poured over it, and it was set ablaze. As it burnt, all present took off their upper garments to show their reverence, and from a distance cast these and their feather fans and parasols as additional fuel into the fire. After the cremation was over, they collected the remains over which to build a stupa. Fahsien did not reach Simhala in time to see this Arhat in the flesh, but he witnessed his funeral ceremony.

The king, being an earnest believer in Buddhism, desired to build a new monastery for the monks. First of all he summoned a great assembly of monks and offered them a splendid feast. After offerings had been made he selected a pair of his best oxen, and adorned their horns with gold, silver and other precious objects. Then he himself ploughed the four sides of a plot of land with a fine golden plough, and ceded this land to the monks, with all the inhabitants, fields and houses on it. An iron title-deed was engraved and given them, to be handed down from generation to generation, for none would dare alter or annul it.

50. A Sermon Preached by an Indian Monk

While in this country Fa-hsien heard an Indian monk, seated on his high seat, deliver the following sermon:

"Buddha's alms-bowl, which was first at Vaisali, is now at Gandhara. After several centuries (Fa-hsien heard the monk mention a definite period of time but he has forgotten the exact number of years stated), it will go to the country of Western Sakas; after several more centuries it will go to the Kingdom of Khotan; after several more centuries it will go to the Kingdom of Kucha; after several more centuries it will go to China, where it will remain for several more centuries before going to Simhala; and after several more centuries it will return to Central India. After having returned to Central India, it will ascend to the Tusita Heaven, where the Maitreya Bodhisattva on seeing it will exclaim:

" 'The alms-bowl of Sakyamuni Buddha has arrived!'

"Then together with all the devas, he will offer flowers and incense to it for seven days. After the seven days it will return to Jambudvipa, where the king of the sea-dragons will carry it to his dragon-palace for safe keeping until Maitreya Bodhisattva is about to become a Buddha. The bowl will then be divided into four and returned to its original place on Mount Vinataka.* After Maitreya's accession to Buddha-hood, the four celestial kings will worship him in the same way as the former Buddhas. The thousand Buddhas of the *Bhadra-kalpa* all use this same alms-bowl. When this bowl vanishes, Buddhism will gradually disappear; and after it has disappeared, the life span of human beings will diminish to as little as five or ten years. By that time there will be no more rice or butter, and men will have grown so savage that even a piece of wood will serve as a weapon in their hands for injury and slaughter. Those who have done good deeds may escape to the mountains to avoid destruction, and come out again after all the evil-doers have killed themselves.

" 'Man's life was once long,' they will say to each other. 'But as men were guilty of many sins and committed all manner of crimes, our life has been shortened to no more than ten years. Therefore let us all do good together and, with charity in our hearts, cultivate virtue and righteousness.'

"Thus all will believe and conduct themselves with propriety, till by degrees their life span is lengthened to as many as 80,000 years. Then Maitreya Bodhisattva will be born into the world. When he begins to expound the Law he will first convert the followers

---

*When Buddha first attained Buddha-hood, each of the four celestial kings presented him with an alms-bowl, and he combined the four into one. After Buddha's Nirvana this bowl became four again, and returned to Mount Vinataka.

and monks of the Law bequeathed by Sakyamuni Buddha, and those who make offerings to the Three Precious Gems, take refuge in Buddha, Dharma and Sangha and observe the Five or the Eight Precepts. The second and third groups will be those who are fit to be saved."

Fa-hsien at that time wished to copy down this sermon.

"There is no written record," said the monk. "I deliver it orally only."

51. The Home-bound Voyage

Fa-hsien stayed in this country for two years, and obtained a copy of the *Rules of the Mahisasakas*. He also procured a copy of the *Dirghagama*, the *Samyuktagama*, and the *Sannipata*, all of which were unknown in China.

Having obtained these Sanskrit books, he set sail on a large merchant ship which carried about two hundred passengers. A small boat trailed behind, for use in case the large vessel should be wrecked, as sailing on this sea was most hazardous. They had sailed eastward with a fair wind for two days only, when they were caught up in a typhoon and the ship sprang a leak, through which the water rushed in. The merchants wanted to take to the smaller boat; but the men already in it severed the cable, for fear lest they be swamped. Then the terrified merchants believed their end was at hand, and in an endeavour to stop the ship from sinking they threw their coarser merchandise into the sea. Fa-hsien also cast overboard his pitcher, wash-basin and some other possessions. Dreading lest the merchants should throw his sacred books and drawings of images into the sea, he invoked Avalokitesvara in all sincerity, as well as the monks of China who had embraced the faith.

"I have come so far to search for the Law," he prayed. "Carry me back with your spiritual power to my destination!"

The hurricane lasted for thirteen days and nights, but finally they reached the shore of an island. When the tide ebbed, they found the leak and repaired it, then sailed on again.

That sea is infested with pirates, and none who meet them can escape alive. The great ocean stretches on every side without end, and one cannot tell east from west. Only by looking at the sun, the moon and the stars, can mariners tell their direction. On dull or rainy days, their vessel simply drifted before the wind. On dark nights, all they could see were great billows beating one against the other and shining like fire, with huge turtles, sea monsters and other amazing creatures in them. The bewildered seamen did not know in what direction they were sailing, but since the ocean was unfathomable there was nowhere to cast anchor; so not until the weather cleared could they distinguish the direction and set the right course. Had they happened to strike a reef, they would have been lost. After voyaging in this way for about ninety days, they reached the country called Yavadvipa.

52. The Country of Yavadvipa

In this country heretical Brahmanism flourishes, and there are very few Buddhists.

After staying here for five months, Fa-hsien embarked on another great merchant ship which also carried about two hundred men. They provided themselves with fifty days' provisions, and set sail on the sixteenth day of the fourth month. Fa-hsien observed the summer retirement on board this vessel, which sailed towards the northeast, bound for Kwangchow.

After sailing for about one month, at the second watch one night it suddenly blew a black squall, and the rain pelted down. Sailors and passengers alike were terror-struck. Once more Fa-hsien in all sincerity invoked Avalokitesvara and the monks in China, and thanks to their protection he was able to live through that night. When day broke, the Brahmans took counsel together.

"It is because we have a Buddhist monk on board," they said, "that we have been so unlucky and suffered so many hardships. We should put him ashore on an island. Why should we risk our lives for the sake of one man?"

Then Fa-hsien's patron spoke up.

"If you want to put this monk ashore," he said, "you will have to put me ashore too, or kill me first. If you leave him on an island, I shall certainly report it to the king when I arrive in China. And you know the king of China also believes in Buddhism and respects monks."

On hearing this, the merchants hesitated, and did not dare to set Fa-hsien ashore.

Owing to the continuous rain, the pilot charted a wrong course. Thus they sailed for more than seventy days till their provisions and water were nearly exhausted. They had to use salt water from the sea for cooking, and each man's ration of fresh water was two pints. Soon the fresh water was nearly used up, and the seamen took counsel together.

"Usually," they said, "it takes only fifty days to reach Kwangchow. But we have been sailing now for many more days than that. We must have been off our course." So they steered towards the northwest to look for land.

53. The Arrival at Laoshan

After twelve days and nights, they landed at the southern shore of Laoshan in Changkuang Prefecture, where they obtained good water and vegetables. After so many dangerous and difficult days and so much anxiety and fear, at last they had reached the shore where, seeing the *li hao*,* they knew that they were in China! They did not know their whereabouts, however, for they saw neither inhabitants nor any trace of man. Some said that they had not yet reached Kwangchow, others that they must have passed it; but no one knew exactly where they were. Accordingly, some sailors rowed into the harbour in the small boat to look for someone to tell them what place this was. They brought back two hunters to the ship, and asked Fa-hsien to act as interpreter. Having reassured the hunters, he questioned them slowly.

"Who are you?" he asked.

"We are Buddhists," they replied.

"What are you looking for in these mountains?"

"Since tomorrow is the fifteenth day of the seventh month, we are trying to find some peaches to offer to Buddha."

"What country is this?"

"This is Changkuang Prefecture in Chingchow. It is under the rule of the House of Liu."

When the merchants heard this, they were delighted, and they begged some men to send their goods to Changkuang. Upon learning that a monk had arrived from across the sea with sacred books and images, Li Yi, the prefect of Changkuang, who was a Buddhist himself, sent men to the shore to carry the

---

Chenopodium album, or goose-foot, a common wild vegetable in China.

scriptures and images to the prefectural city. Then the merchants returned to Yangchow. Meanwhile Liu Tao-lien* had arrived at Chingchow, and he entertained Fa-hsien for a winter and a summer. After the summer retirement, Fa-hsien, who had long been away from his fellow monks, desired to return to Changan; but since his business was of such importance, he travelled southward to Chienkang, the southern capital, where he met a fellow monk** to whom he showed the books of monastic discipline.

54. The Conclusion

Fa-hsien started his journey from Changan and spent six years on the way to the Middle Kingdom, where he stayed for six years; and he spent three years on his return journey before he reached Chingchow. He travelled through nearly thirty countries, from the west of the Desert to the land of India. No complete account can be given of the excellent conduct and religious teaching of the monks he met on his journey; but it was to inform the monks in China of these things that Fa-hsien crossed the seas at the risk of his humble life, and braved many hardships and dangers to return home. Thanks to the spiritual protection of the Three Precious Gems, he was able to come safely through many perils. So he has put down this outline

---

*The second brother of Liu Yu, who later became emperor.
**The Indian monk Buddhabhadra.

of his travels on bamboo and silk, in order that the devout may share all his experiences. This was in the cyclic year of Chia Yin.*

Postscript by Another Monk

It was at the end of the summer retirement in the twelfth year of the era of Yi Hsi of the Tsin dynasty, and the year of Canopus,** that we welcomed the venerable Fa-hsien. While he remained with us, preaching, we questioned him again about his travels, and found that he was an unassuming, affable man, who answered truthfully. We therefore urged him to give a more detailed account of what he had previously narrated so briefly. Thus he related his story once more from beginning to end.

"When I look back on what I have been through," he said, "my heart begins to pound and I start to sweat. I risked all those dangers with no thought for myself, because I had a fixed purpose and, simple as I am, was single-minded. That was why I embarked upon a journey in which death seemed almost certain, and I had one chance only in ten thousand of surviving."

We were moved by what he said. Such men as this are rare whether in ancient times or at the present day. Since the Great Religion travelled east, there has been no one to equal Fa-hsien in his selfless search

---

*A.D. 414.
**A.D. 416.

for the Law. From this we may know that all things are possible to the sincere of heart, and all things can be accomplished if a man has determination. For is it not true that he succeeded because he disregarded what others value, and valued what others disregard?